DISCOVER NEW ZEALAND

Nature Lore of the Maori

**photographs
GORDON ELL**

**compiled by
PITA GRAHAM**

**THE BUSH PRESS
OF AUCKLAND**

BIRTH OF THE WORLD

The 70 children of Earth and Sky pushed them apart to end the ages of darkness and let in the world of light.

Into the world of light

For a thousand ages there was darkness in the world. Earth and Sky clung so close to each other that there was no light.

Their many children, lying between, grew restless in this world of night. They struggled to push the Earth and Sky apart. As they succeeded the world was flooded with light. From there the natural world took shape.

The plants and animals of New Zealand are descended from the gods. The sky, Rangi, is their ancestral Father. Papa, the earth, is their Mother.

The children of Earth and Sky fathered all creatures that followed.

It was Tane, god of forests, who finally thrust his parents apart by stretching his arms up against the sky.

Tangaroa took the waters, as god of the sea.

Rongo became god of the cultivated food, the garden crops.

Haumia became god of the foods that grow in the wild.

Tawhiri was angry that his brothers had forced Earth and Sky apart. He fought his brothers, becoming god of winds and storms.

Ruaumoko hid in the belly of the Earth, as god of the volcanoes.

It was Tu, the god of war, who stood and fought.

In the world of light the winds and storms still fight the realms of land and sea. People fight with these elements to survive. Yet the bounty of sea and land also provides them with food.

Maori nature lore is about the uses that people make of this natural world.

Tane placed the sun in the sky and established the world of light. He fought against Whiro, the spirit of darkness, through the heavens and the earth. The conflict between light and darkness is as old as time.

Having thrust apart Earth and Sky, Tane found the world only dimly lit. He placed Marama the moon and her family of stars, the whanau marama, in the body of Rangi, the Sky Father above. The positions of heavenly bodies mark the seasons for planting and harvest.

EARTH AND SKY APART

Ranginui, the Sky Father, is set apart from the Earth Mother by the lifting force of Tane in the form of a tree. Floods rise about the body of Papa as Rangi mourns their separation. Engravings from *Te Tohunga* by W. Dittmer, 1907.

THE FIRST LIGHT

The first light to be glimpsed by the children of Rangi and Papa was but a glimmer - the dim light of Moko huruhuru, the glow-worm. The delicate flowers of the clambering clematis, Puawananga, like stars in the forest, were among the first to see the light.

Living off the Land

The first New Zealanders arrived on the shores of Aotearoa perhaps a thousand years ago. They were Polynesian people, sea-farers, whose ancestors had explored and settled the tropical South Pacific islands over some 2000 years. Their late discovery of New Zealand, far in the southwest corner of the great ocean of Kiwa, revealed a new kind of land.

The place was cooler and much larger than their tropical islands, and the plants and animals were different. For people who relied on the products of land and sea for food and shelter, the new land was an urgent challenge. To survive they had to make a new way of life and find new foods.

In Aotearoa the Polynesian voyagers developed a new culture. They explored the coasts and the forests and found new foods and materials. They developed new ways of making traditional clothes and tools. Gradually, over several hundred years, the population grew as the Polynesians spread through the land and founded new tribes.

These people developed what is known today as Maori culture. Yet they never forgot their ancestry in the tropical Pacific. Traditional tales and myths trace back to those earlier times, when the gods and demi-gods created the natural world on which they relied for their survival.

The Wrath of Ruaumoko

Ruaumoko was the youngest child of the Earth and Sky. He was still being suckled by the Earth when Tane forced his parents apart.

As Sky and Earth were separated the tears of Rangi rained down on the body of his wife Papa. There was snow and hail. The waters flooded the land and left little for their children.

To lessen the tears of Rangi and save the Earth, some of their sons turned their Mother over to face the underworld. Now the grief of Rangi was lessened for he could not see the face of his wife. The tears of Rangi fell on the back of Papa and the answering mists, rising from her valleys, shrouded and protected the Earth.

Ruaumoko, however, was now underneath his Mother, where it was cold. His brothers arranged for him to have fire to keep warm. Yet he was angry, buried deep below the Earth, in darkness. So he retaliated with the sacred fires which erupted through the skin of his Mother, as volcanoes and geysers and mudpools on the body of the Earth. When Ruaumoko moved beneath his Mother the Earth shook in earthquakes.

So Ruaumoko shaped the land.

ACTIVE VOLCANOES

Volcanoes and earthquakes are constant reminders of Ruaumoko hidden beneath the Earth Mother. Tarawera, which last exploded in 1886, is on a line to the Tongariro volcanoes in the south and White Island in the north. This view looks over the Bay of Plenty from Tarawera and shows dormant Putauaki (Mt Edgecumbe) and Whakaari (White Island) steaming on the horizon 80 kilometres away.

Ruaumoko's anger is expressed in a line of active volcanoes stretching through the central North Island and out through the Bay of Plenty to the Pacific "ring of fire." Movement of earth plates along this fault produces frequent earthquakes and varied volcanic activity such as mudpools, geysers, hot pools and fumaroles.

VOLCANIC MUDPOOLS

The central North Island has many volcanic places which show Ruaumoko's anger. These mudpools are near Rotorua.

The Shaping of the Earth

The steep and broken hills of New Zealand were created when the demi-god Maui fished up the North Island.

The deeds of Maui are known throughout Polynesia. It was he who led his brothers to net the sun and beat it so its course became slow and long through the sky. He later stole fire from his ancestress. Maui even turned his brother-in-law, Irawaru, into a dog because he was jealous of his luck at fishing.

Perhaps it was not surprising that his brothers were reluctant to take him fishing with them. At length Maui got to sea by hiding under the floorboards of their canoe. Off-shore he revealed himself then led them to a good but distant fishing ground. Yet still they would not give him any bait for fishing with his enchanted hook.

So Maui bloodied his own nose and used it to bait the hook. When he fished up the North Island it was smooth and flat. They beached their boat upon it, but Maui asked his brothers not to eat the fish or cut it up until he could find a priest to bless the new land and offer a portion to the gods. While he was gone to arrange the ceremonies his brothers disobeyed him. They began to cut up the fish. Te Ika a Maui - the fish of Maui as the North Island is still known in Maori - writhed and twisted and flapped, thrusting up mountains, forming cliffs and gullies, breaking up the plains.

So the perfect land was broken.

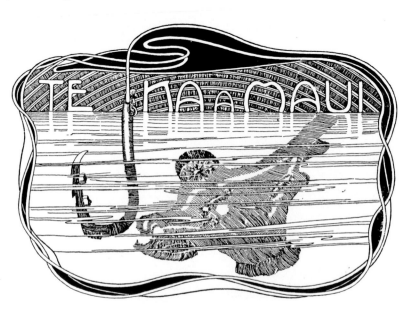

THE FISH OF MAUI

The shape of Te Ika a Maui, the North Island, resembles a skate or stingray with its tail in the Far North and mouth about Wellington Harbour. Curving Cape Kidnappers, at the southern tip of Hawkes Bay, resembles the enchanted hook with which Maui fished up the island.

MAUI'S GIANT CATCH

Maui fishes up the North Island of New Zealand, as pictured by W. Dittmer. Heroic stories of the demigod Maui abound among the Polynesian people of the Pacific.

Maui also stole fire from his ancestor Mahuika. The fire of the goddess was in the nails of her fingers and toes. Maui begged the fire of one nail then put it out. He went back for more fire and extinguished that too. So he begged all her toenails and fingernails but one. When the old lady realised that she had been tricked she threw this last flaming nail on the ground where it set the earth and water on fire. Then, pursued by flames, Maui called on Tawhiri of the storms to bring rain. To save her last fire Mahuika threw a few sparks into the wood of Kaikomako and Whau. Maori make fire by rubbing such hard and soft woods together. (Whau, page 31).

The World of the Polynesians

The Maori traditions of the creation of the world may be heard in many parts of the Pacific. They are part of the heritage of all Polynesians. The story of Maui fishing up the land is told also in Hawaii where he is said to have caught the island called Maui.

Yet, in their New Zealand versions, these tales relate closely to our own natural world. When Maui stole fire from his ancestress, its spirit escaped into the wood of the Kaikomako, which can be used to make fire by rubbing.

Maori nature tales are often about these special qualities of plants and animals. They make up a vast basket of knowledge about the natural world.

Tane, Father of the Forest

Of the seventy offspring of Earth and Sky, Tane is the one who did most to shape the new world of light. He set the stars in their heaven and set up the sun. Tane also journeyed as far as the twelfth heaven and brought back three baskets of knowledge. With the help of several of his brothers he made a woman of clay and breathed life into her.

As Tane-mahuta he fathered the forest, creating the trees and insects and birds. The children of Tane are many and their offspring are vital to the Maori, who depended on them for food, materials and shelter.

KAURI FOREST

The Kauri tree grows in the warmer north of New Zealand and is used for canoes. The tree produces a gum which gave rise to an early European industry, the harvest of the gum for making such varied items as linoleum and cosmetics. Maori used the gum as something to chew. Burnt, it produced the black powder which coloured moko or tattoo designs.

THE CHIEFLY TREES

The giant trees of the forest were regarded as chiefs; the smaller as commoners. Special ceremony attended the felling of a forest giant for use as a canoe.

Totara was the most respected for it lasted long and was used for canoes, carving and structural timbers. Even its bark found use, as it could be tied into the shape of a basket for carrying fluids.

The great trees served as a home and feeding place for birds. All were known as the children of Tane though several of his lesser-known brothers and offspring had a hand in populating the forest.

Because of their relationship with Tane, the Maori felt at home in the forest. Some people still trace their family back to a forest ancestor, perhaps a bird like the Kokako or a great tree.

Maori nature lore included knowing when the forest giants and the smaller plants were in flower and fruit. In such seasons hunters gathered to harvest the visiting birds.

Many of the shrubs and vines provided food and useful materials.

BELOW The Karaka has a highly poisonous berry but Maori developed ways of treating it as a meal.

The Fight Between Land and Sea

When Earth and Sky separated, Tawhiri father of winds and storms set upon his brothers, felling trees in the kingdom of Tane and whipping up vast and angry seas where Tangaroa was hiding.

The fish and the reptiles at first hid together in the forests of Tane to escape Tawhiri's anger. Then they began to argue in fear at the assault of the wild weather. Ikatere, the father of fish, thought he could find more shelter for his offspring in the oceans of Tangaroa. Tutewehiwehi, father of reptiles, wanted to flee inland. Their children argued too, at last separating into two parties, one going to the sea and one staying on land.

This created jealousy between Tane, father of the land creatures, and Tangaroa, father of the sea creatures.

Because the reptiles stayed on land, Tangaroa has waged war on his brother Tane ever since. Tangaroa has beaten at the shores, swallowing land and washing away trees with their families of birds and insects. Tangaroa also uses the waves to swallow canoes, which are made from the sons of Tane.

Yet Tane has fought back too. He has given to his brother Tu, father of warlike man, the trees to build canoes, and the fibres and bones with which to fashion nets and fish hooks. So he has revenge as Tu's people harvest the sea creatures, the children of Tangaroa.

The fight between sea and land continues to this day as angry seas assail the coast and flooded rivers carve away the hills and plains.

The Revenge of Fierce Man

The last of the storm god's battles was with Tu, the form of Fierce Man. One of the last children of Earth and Sky, it was Tu alone who had wanted to kill his parents. His brothers decided otherwise, forcing them apart instead, to let in the light. Yet Tu remained angry as befits the god of war.

When Tawhiri flooded the new earth and defeated his brothers, Tu alone stood firm. The fierce youngster turned on the winds and storms, driving them back to the bosom of Rangi, their father in the heavens. Then he turned on his brothers for their cowardice.

First Tu defeated Tane and the creatures of the forests. He made nooses from leaves and set traps for the birds and other creatures among the branches of the forest. In this way he took away from Tane some of his authority, the mana of the birds and plants. By destroying the tapu which protected them, Tu made such creatures common and available for eating. Then he turned his vengeance on Tangaroa's offspring. This battle too he won, making nets from flax and catching the fish from the waters. So the creatures of the sea were made common too and available for the use of people.

Tu then sought out the offspring of his brothers Rongo of the sweet potato kumara and Haumia of the bracken fern. He found the shoots rising where these plants had hidden in the body of Papa, the Earth Mother. Digging up fern root and kumara he ate these too, making them common and food for people.

Tu could not, however, defeat Tawhiri. So while four of his famous brothers now serve him as a source of food and materials, Tawhiri of the winds and storms remains an enemy, hidden in the bosom of the sky. To this day, the winds and storms continue to assail the descendants of Tu, attempting to destroy us by land and sea.

LIZARDS

Maori feared the lizard, as it was often a form in which a god appeared. The lizard was sometimes a guardian of the mauri, or life force, of the forest.

The Gifts of Tane

The realm of Tane provided for many of the Maori needs. There were trees for canoes and huts. Many trees and shrubs produced berries to eat. They also attracted birds for the hunter. Insects and their grubs were gathered as food.

Vines and leaves could be used for tying and making nets. Maori knew the qualities of different plants for making fabric and mats. Some plants provided dyes and medicine too.

WEKA or WOODHEN
The Weka was a popular food because it could be preserved in its own fat and eaten later. William Fox pictured his Maori guide Kehu, catching weka with a noose, during an expedition to the Nelson Lakes.

ALEXANDER TURNBULL LIBRARY

CHILDREN OF PUNGA

Insects belong to Tane. Maori thought insects ugly, the offspring of Punga, yet they ate them. The grubs of huhu beetles were popular.

Some insects embodied the spirit of ugliness. The Giant Weta Punga was named for its parent. The Cave Weta was respected as an underground spirit. This one sits by a rare Maori rock carving in a forest cave.

14

Living with Nature

The first settlers in New Zealand were hunters and fisherfolk, people who harvested the natural products of coast and forest. Through the seasons they wandered in search of food, finding the forest fruits and harvesting the birds and insects, fish and various seafoods, when these were most plentiful.

In doing so, Maori built up a store of local knowledge about nature and the outdoors. Without such knowledge the people could not have survived. For nature provided not only food but the materials for clothing, shelter and tools.

The people were aware that their lives also depended on saving some food for tomorrow. Food was taken as a gift of the gods, who allowed their children to be eaten. They were harvested with respect. Laws of tapu and rahui limited the taking of certain animals and plants to special seasons.

The nature lore of the Maori includes a knowledge of the place of the gods and spirits in guarding their creatures. Karakia or prayers should be recited before the hunt or the harvest. The spirits of forest and seashore must be addressed before the lives of their offspring are taken.

RATA IN FLOWER

Southern Rata in flower in summer. Rata produces a honey which Maori could gather by draining the flowers into a bowl. More often rata served as a bait tree for birds in search of the nectar. Flocks of the bush parrot Kaka would gather at these and other flowering trees in season. The birds were snared or speared (see over page and on cover).

Hunting Forest Birds

The native pigeon, known as Kereru or Kuku, and the Kaka parrot were favourite foods. Birds were hunted with spears or caught in a noose. To attract the kaka, Maori kept pet birds, secured by a leg ring to a trap or target area. Their calls would bring down inquisitive wild birds to be killed or caught. Ground-dwelling birds, such as Weka and Kiwi, could be hunted with dogs.

CATCHING WILD BIRDS

At bottom left, pigeons gather on a tree where troughs of water are surrounded by snares.
Below, a hunter hiding under fern leaves is using a decoy Kaka to attract wild birds close enough to spear.

CATCHING WILD DUCKS

Native ducks gathered in huge numbers at moulting time. Without their flight feathers they were easier to catch. The hunter, wearing a camouflage of foliage, swims up to the birds and takes them from below.

PIGEON SNARING

In the heat of summer birds are drawn to pools of water. This time the hunter has set the snares on the ground to catch thirsty pigeons.

FOOD FROM THE SHORE

Rocky reefs and mudflats are a valuable source of kaimoana. Women collected shellfish and seaweeds on the shore.

Children of Tangaroa

On the reefs and mudflats, Maori people gather kaimoana, the food of the sea. The creatures include Kina or sea eggs, various shellfish, even tasty seaweeds. Maori rights to take food from the coast are still guarded by tribes.

Many different shellfish were eaten. The rocky shore produced snails large and small, including the little Pupu or periwinkle. The mussel was an important food. From the muddy shores of estuaries and the beach sands came the bivalves: cockles, Pipi, Tuatua and Toheroa.

In the old days, fishermen would net from the shore or go to sea in canoes and fish with lines of flax and hooks of bone or shell. The sea also provided more bounty in the shape of a whale or seal.

EDIBLE SHELLFISH

The native rock oyster is found in the north of the North Island. Since the 1960s, the much larger Pacific rock oyster has taken over from the native species. The Pacific oyster is said to have been brought to our coasts on the hulls of Japanese vessels. They have a greater tolerance of tidal movements and, being more successful, have largely smothered the native species.

CLUES FROM THE PAST

Midden or rubbish dump from ancient times reveals what Maori ate from the sea. Some midden contain shells no longer found nearby. Other times the size of the shells show a change in the health of harbour or reef. Sites were left when the take of sea foods became less and the area given time to recover.

USES OF PAUA

Paua, an abalone, was valued for its food and for its colouring. Now heavily reduced in number, paua is still harvested for feasts though it is hard to find within a day's drive of any major towns. When the coarse pink shell is ground away the glowing colours of the paua are revealed. Maori used the shell as a flashing lure when fishing and to form the eyes on carvings and ornaments.

Between Land and Sea

Where land meets sea, on the tidal mudflats, flocks of migratory birds gather. Many thousands still flock to the great harbours of New Zealand, particularly in summer, when they come from as far away as the sub-Arctic regions of Siberia and North America to feed. Such bounty was a traditional source of food for the Maori. Nets and nooses were set up in favourite feeding places. Then birds were frightened into them.

So vast were the flocks that birds could be literally beaten from the skies. Even today it is possible to see flocks of many hundreds swooping low to find a resting place when the high tide drives the birds from the mudflats. Maori hunters would position themselves on favoured bird roosts, or along the course of the flyways where birds swooped low from one roost to another.

Birds were preserved in their own fat.

HUNTING SHORE BIRDS

Flocks of godwit can still be seen feeding on harbour mudflats and estuaries in summer. As the tide rises they swoop up in great flocks and move to drier ground. Here Maori hunters have positioned themselves on a natural flight path. As the birds swoop low, Maori beat them from the sky with branches.

20

SNARING BIRDS

Wading birds like the Kuaka (godwit) and Poaka (stilt) may gather in hundreds on the mudflats where they feed. As the tide rises they are driven to higher ground. Maori set snares on the sandbanks at low tide. When the birds were driven onto the sandbanks, by rising water, they could be frightened into the snares.

ABOVE Pied stilts gather on an islet as the tide rises, beneath a Maori hunting snare.

BELOW Godwit and other wading birds are driven towards snares by the rising tide.

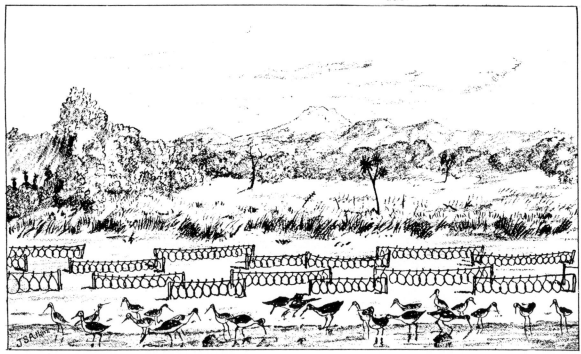

Sea Mammals

Whales and seals were classed by Maori as creatures in the care of Tangaroa, the god of sea life. They were once much more common off the coasts of New Zealand. The bones of seals and whales are found in the rubbish tips and remains of ancient camp fires left by Maori about the coast. Whalebone also provided a material for carving weapons, such as the kotiate club, ornaments like the rei puta, and for making cloak pins and combs.

FUR SEALS

Once abundant on the New Zealand coast, fur seals were harvested to the verge of extinction by early sealers from Europe.

MUTTONBIRDS

Sooty shearwaters, the Titi of the south, are still harvested by Maori on a few offshore islands. Once muttonbird species also nested on the mainland, some as far inland as the slopes of Tongariro and Lake Waikaremoana. Muttonbirds are packed in kelp bags and preserved in their own fat.

Picture at left shows two of the family of petrels and shearwaters found around the New Zealand coast. The mottled petrel (top) was once found on the mainland but is now restricted to southern islands. Bulier's shearwater (bottom) nests at the Poor Knights Islands off Northland.

CATCHING INANGA

The young of the freshwater fish Inanga are also known as whitebait. The tiny fish ran in the rivers in their millions before the draining of their breeding grounds in the tidal estuaries. Maori netted Inanga in spring, drying them for later use.

Bounty of Lakes and River

Tangaroa's children occupy the waterways of the land as well. Lamprey and eel were taken in trap and pot. In season whole families would move to a trapping place where the migrating fish were taken.

Whitebait, the family of Inanga, are a delicacy to most New Zealanders. Maori trapped the adults as the fish went down to the lower reaches of the rivers to breed. They caught the little whitebait as the young fish returned to the rivers from the estuaries, to migrate upstream.

Crabs and crayfish (Koura) are popular sea foods. The koura, too, has a freshwater form, found beneath stones. They can be fished for with baited traps but lures of branches placed in the water will also ensnare them.

The freshwater mussel can still be found in healthy streams and lakes. Its meat was eaten but the shell was also valued as a knife for cutting. Sharp edges of the shell would slice through flax, severing the strong leaves. Then the shell edge was used to scrape apart the fibres for drying and weaving.

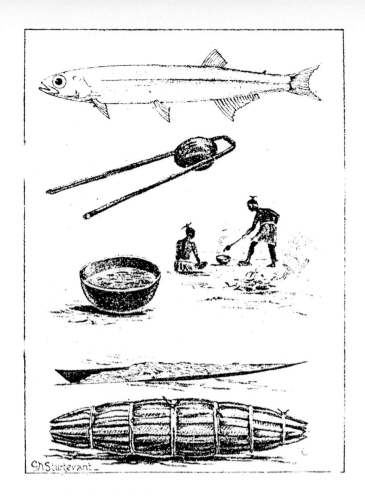

PRESERVING INANGA

Maori used a cooking and drying technique to preserve whitebait. The mature fish, up to 20cm long, live upstream but come down to the tidal zone to lay their eggs. Their hatching fry are caught and quickly cooked before packing in leaves for preserving. The stone was heated in a fire then plunged into the bowl or kumete for cooking. The whitebait were dried before packing.

DRYING FISH

Eels, lampreys, sea fish and whitebait were all dried in the sun or smoked for later use. Fires were set to help along the process of drying (below). Here masses of tiny whitebait are set out on the mats to dry in the sun. Larger fish were hung on racks.

The Hidden Foods

The fathers of wild foods and crops were important offspring of Earth and Sky.

Rongo fathered the crops which were cultivated by Maori - the kumara, yam, gourd and taro.

Haumia fathered the foods that grew naturally and could be gathered from the wild, such as fern root.

When Tawhiri the storm father turned on his brothers in anger he drove Rongo and Haumia to hide underground. The roots of Rongo's garden crops were hidden in the ground and no leaves showed on the surface. The fern roots of Haumia were similarly hidden.

It was Tu who found them, angry that his brothers had hidden instead of fighting the storms. The "hair" of the fern showed above the grasses and Tu dug down to get at the roots. The shoots of kumara and the cultivated plants also showed where they were hiding. Tu made them common and available as food by eating them.

WILD FOODS

Many herbs could be used as green food by Maori. Sow thistle, known as Puha, is still popular. Other foods included native celery and spinach. Maori diets expanded greatly when early European explorers brought their vegetables and fruit, pigs and chickens.

ARUHE or FERN ROOT

The roots of bracken fern were a staple food of the ancient Maori. Forests were burned to create the open country it requires. The fern leaves are the "hair" of the plant which led the angry Tu to find where his brother Haumia had hidden his roots underground.

Wooden beaters were used to hammer the starchy food out of the fern root. Mixed with water this starch made a floury paste which could be baked into a hard cake.

The Garden Plants

The Polynesians introduced several plants to New Zealand. Maori traditions tell of the foods carried on the canoes. These include the taro, the yam, the gourd, a tropical form of cabbage tree, and the kumara or sweet potato.

Taro still grows in the warm creeks and ponds of northern New Zealand, though the plants are usually of more modern varieties, introduced last century.

Yams and gourds (Hue) were so difficult to grow in the colder climate of Aotearoa that special stone piles were made in the fields to gather the warmth of the sun to ripen the fruit. While both were food, gourds were especially important for they could also be dried as vessels to carry food or water. Maori had no pottery and so had to carry things in woven baskets, bark containers, or hollowed wood.

The tropical cabbage tree or Ti provided shoots and roots, rich in natural sugars. This species, Cordyline terminalis, is extinct now in the wild, its form too delicate to resist browsing animals such as possum.

The kumara, or sweet potato, originates in South America but has become the staple vegetable of many warmer countries around the Pacific. The vegetable is still popular with New Zealanders but the crops planted today are modern varieties, producing much more food than the original plants brought from Polynesia.

The garden plants of Rongo were grown near settlements but the people still made journeys away to hunt or fish, and to gather wild food.

TI - THE CABBAGE TREES

Ti-kouka, the common cabbage tree of New Zealand, was valued as a source of food and materials by the early Maori. Its strong leaves were used to tie up bundles and frameworks, and sometimes to decorate fabrics when dyed. Roots of ti-kouka were dug up and cooked in big pits to produce a roasted starch called kauru. The shoots and flowers of ti-kouka were also eaten in season.

In Maori lore, an early and profuse flowering of the cabbage tree is said to predict a long, hot summer. In recent years many ti-kouka have flowered well and died, owing to a bacteria which grows in its roots, poisoning the plant. Thus a tree once widespread on the islands of New Zealand is being rapidly reduced in number.

Animal skins, meat and bones

The islands of New Zealand were torn from the ancient continents before the evolution of mammals. Animals and plants developed, isolated from other islands by the great ocean of Kiwa.

New Zealand has no native land mammals except for two tiny bats. These were the offspring of Pekapeka.

The dog, kuri, was brought to New Zealand by the Maori. So was the Polynesian rat, the kiore. Both were food for the Maori.

The kuri descends from Irawaru, the brother-in-law of Maui, whom that trickster turned into a dog. Maori used kuri to seek out the flightless birds which had grown unafraid in a land without hunters. The skin of the kuri was bound into flaxen capes worn by chiefs. The bones and teeth of the dog made personal decorations and tools. Its flesh could be eaten.

DOG SKIN CLOAK
Dog skin cloaks were highly valued by the old-time Maori. This was the best way to turn away rain, hail and snow.

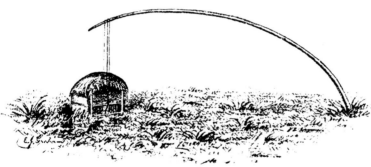

KIORE TRAP

Kiore were trapped for food. These small rats feed largely on seeds and some insects and eggs. They would invade a settlement too and Maori placed their pataka food stores on poles so the rats could not get in. This kind of rat has vanished now from the mainland but many survive on offshore islands where they are free from the competition of the stronger rats introduced on European ships.

KIWI HUNT BY NIGHT

A hunting dog accompanies its owner in preparation for a Kiwi hunt by night. Branches are twisted over to mark the path of the hunt. Moonlight reflected from the silvery underleaf of species like the silver fern could help Maori find their way at night. Dogs led the hunters to the kiwi as it emerged at night to feed.

CALABASHES

This sketch shows a totara bark carrier and two carved gourds. The Maori had no pottery so calabashes like these served as containers. Sometimes the scoop of a nikau branch was used as a carrier. Hollow stones and wooden carved bowls were also used in place of the pottery or metal containers used by other cultures.

Shelter from Nature

While Tawhiri sent cold winds and storms, the riches of the natural world of Tane supplied the means of shelter and clothing.

Maori used the resources of the forest for their buildings. Tree trunks and foliage provided frames and thatching. Nikau leaves provided the roof. Often huts were dug into the ground for further shelter from the winds.

Lashings to tie the frames together could be made from fibrous plants like flax and Kiekie. Such materials could also be tied into mats or formed into baskets or cloaks. Most people wore only a maru or apron of flax, though that material could also be fashioned into rain capes for colder weather. Sandals were also woven for walking on rough ground.

In earlier times, flax was grown in plantations as a source for the ropes which bound canoes and buildings, and for the weaving of fishing nets and traps.

Some wild shrubs too had special uses. Hangehange, the scrambling vine, could be bent to frame nets and baskets. The matagouri shrub, Tutumakuri, has sharp needles which were used in some places as needles for tattooing.

Maori found rich bounty in the forest.

MAORI MEDICINES
The roots of Harakeke (right) provided a concoction to end constipation. The leaves provided a fibre for dressing and binding wounds. The leaves of Koromiko and the nuts of Manuka were employed to stop diarrhoea.

Medicines from Nature

The causes of disease were the offspring of Whiro, the spirit of darkness and enemy of Tane who brought the light. These spirits dwelt in the darkness below the earth and each had an affliction which could take up residence in the human body.

The ancient Maori fought these effects of breaking the laws of tapu, with the magic of the priest or tohunga. Diseases were not to be treated; rather the devils had to be removed, then treatment was given to cure the illness. Some were absorbed by moss, others by the leaves of coprosma species, like Karamu. Tane's children were also used as herbal remedies.

Sometimes aromatic green leaves were used to make a steam bath. Such leaves were laid over hot stones, as in a hangi oven, generating steam to be breathed or wafted over an afflicted body. The large leaves of Rangiora and Pukapuka were used to bandage wounds. The leaves of other plants were burned to an ash to dress ulcers and soothe burns. Flax was used to bind.

SYMBOL OF LIFE
The underneath of the Rangiora leaf is silvery in colour. When waved by dancers, it symbolises life.

SYMBOL OF DEATH
Kawakawa, the northern pepper plant, sometimes symbolises death and may be carried by women mourners at a funeral.

HARAKEKE

Flax was valuable as a source of fibre, for ropes and weaving. To keep a good supply, Maori grew it as a crop in swamps. The flowers produce a honey which was sucked out with a straw and used to attract the Tui birds, which were snared or speared.

Kiekie and cabbage tree also produced valuable fibres.

PINGAO

On the beach, Pingao grass produced fine yellow thread. It is used for tying up panels of taniko work and also to colour kete bags.

WHAU

This soft, light wood is a close relative of the paper mulberry which the Maori introduced to make a kind of tapa cloth. The plants died in the cold. Whau was useful for making net floats. Dry shavings of the soft wood were rubbed with the harder wood of Kaikomako to make fire.

The Untouched Islands

Before the first Polynesian explorers came to New Zealand no humans had ever landed. The isolated islands were clad in dense forest, with extensive wetlands, swamps and rivers. There were flightless birds, like the Moa, standing up to four metres high. Among the animals was a survivor from the age of dinosaurs, the reptilian Tuatara. Trees and plants took unusual forms. Nothing could protect the land from the impact of its first settlers.

The Maori changed the nature of New Zealand by hunting and by clearing the land. Within a few hundred years some seventeen different kinds of bird became extinct, many of them flightless and unable to escape the skill of hunters.

The Fires of Tamatea which raged in the South Island during the fourteenth century are often claimed to have begun as a way of clearing the land to make it easier to hunt moa. In other places the forests were burned to clear ground for the bracken fern. The hillsides around Maori settlements then became a source of fern root, a staple food in the colder places where kumara and taro would not grow.

By the time European settlers arrived the forests had been trimmed back to 80% of the land; now not yet 200 years later, the natural lands have shrunk to 40% of their virgin state. Foreign weeds and pests, introduced wild animals and insects have changed our natural world completely. Some of the natural treasures of the old-time Maori are now rare and endangered.

Yet the traditions of Maori nature lore survive. Kaimoana, the food from the sea, is popular with New Zealanders of all races and becoming scarce in some places as a result. Tribal rights to take wild food are fiercely guarded, as with the "muttonbird" harvest where certain families may take petrels or titi from burrows on offshore islands. The rights to take native plants from Crown forests for "cultural purposes" are still practised, whether it be a tree for the hull of a canoe, or some fruits to make dyes, or materials for traditional weaving.

Maori culture evolved in New Zealand as a way of living closely with our natural world. Not surprisingly therefore, nature lore remains a living part of Maori culture today.

FLAX RAIN CAPE
Maori usually wore only a small flax apron or maro. A cape like this was worn to turn away extreme cold or wet. It is made of tags of Harakeke (flax). Sandals of fibrous leaves, like flax or Ti, were worn when crossing rough places.